TRAVEL TO AMALFI COAST 2024

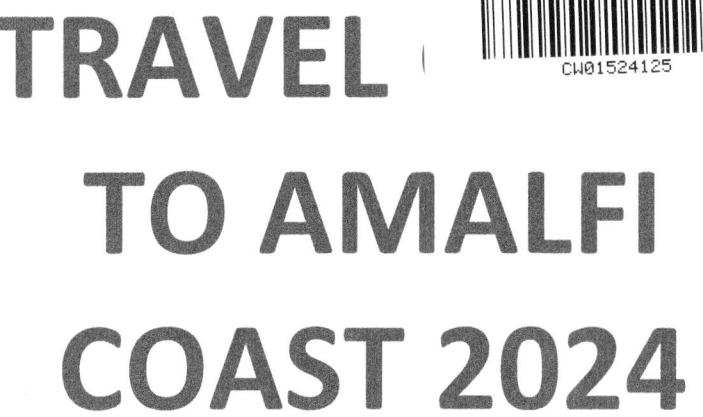
An Easy Guidebook on Everything You Need to Know About Visiting Amalfi Coast, Italy

Megan Peterson

CONTENTS

INTRODUCTION

A Brilliant Day on the Amalfi Coast

As the sun washed the Amalfi Coast in a warm brilliant shine, I ended up remaining on the precipices, entranced by the sheer excellence that unfurled before my eyes. The musical sound of the waves running into the rough coastline made an orchestra that repeated the untamed soul of the Tyrrhenian Ocean.

Positano, with its pastel-tinted structures sticking to the bluffs, was a dream directly from a fantasy. Each step along the winding cobblestone roads uncovered secret shops and curious bistros, where the aroma of newly fermented coffee waited in the air. Local people, with their comforting grins, shared stories that additional profundity to the energetic woven artwork of this beach front asylum.

Ravello, roosted high over the ocean, felt like a peaceful break. The terraced nurseries of Manor Cimbrone unfurled like a living magnum opus, offering all encompassing perspectives that extended into the great beyond. I tracked down comfort in the serenity of this raised retreat, where time appeared to dial back, permitting me to relish each experience.

I was warmly welcomed by Amalfi, the center of the coast. The bustling Piazza del Duomo was alive with activity, and the impressive Cathedral of Saint Andrew stood as a reminder of centuries of rich history. The smell of newly prepared sfogliatella drifted from nearby pastry shops, enticing me to enjoy the district's culinary joys.

As I explored the waterfront trails, the Way of the Divine beings unfurled like a great exhibition. Each step uncovered stunning vistas of the purplish blue ocean underneath, and the air was loaded up with the wonderful fragrance of blossoming wildflowers. It was a trip that tested my actual perseverance as well as compensated me with a feeling of achievement and remarkable magnificence.

I was able to get a different look at the sheer cliffs and hidden grottoes from the deck of a boat by sailing along the coast. The turquoise waters shone under the Mediterranean sun, welcoming me to take a reviving dunk in the ocean. It was a snapshot of unadulterated delight, encompassed by the regular ponders that make the Amalfi Coast a genuine heaven.

As the day unfurled into night, I ended up on a clifftop porch, enjoying a tasty fish supper. The lights of the waterfront towns sparkled underneath, making an enchanted feeling. I gave a toast to the beauty of the Amalfi Coast with a bottle of local wine in my hand. In this place, every moment felt like a brushstroke on the canvas of a perfect day.

The night air conveyed the song of unrecorded music, and I meandered through the limited roads of Positano, where the warm sparkle of lights enlightened the way. The town had changed into a heartfelt safe house, and the personal environment was elevated by the far off sound of chuckling from shoreline eateries.

Ravello, under the delicate light of the moon, took on a supernatural emanation. The notable estates and gardens appeared to wake up with shadows, and the quietness was broken exclusively by a periodic stir of leaves. It was a snapshot of tranquil consideration, offering an unmistakable difference to the enthusiastic scenes of the day.

Back in Amalfi, the night uncovered one more side of the town. The House of prayer of Holy person Andrew was perfectly enlightened, projecting a glorious shine over the Piazza del Duomo. A scene of unparalleled beauty was created as I strolled along the waterfront as the lights' reflections danced on the rippling sea.

The next day brought new undertakings. I was able to take in the vibrant colors and aromas of fresh produce, handmade crafts, and the famous limoncello of the area when I went to a local market. Discussions with the merchants revealed the energy they immersed their manifestations, making each buy a story to be shared upon my return.

Yet again climbing the seaside trails, I experienced secret bays and detached sea shores, welcoming snapshots of isolation and reflection. The ocean breeze conveyed murmurs of antiquated stories, and the rough scene appeared to hold the privileged insights of previous eras. It was an excursion through time, where the at various times consistently interlaced.

I was on a boat to Capri, my final excursion before saying goodbye, as my Amalfi Coast adventure came to an end. The island's popular Blue Cave charmed me with its ethereal sparkle, a fitting illustration for the charm that the Amalfi Coast had given occasion to feel qualms about my spirit.

Pondering my visit, I understood that the Amalfi Coast was in excess of an objective; it was a vivid encounter that connected every one of the faculties. From the visual quality to the culinary enjoyments, the glow of local people to the immortal history, each feature of this beach front diamond made a permanent imprint on my heart.

As the boat diverted me from the Amalfi Coast, I conveyed with me recollections, however a significant appreciation for the creativity of nature, the extravagance of culture, and the delight of finding a spot that feels like a genuine magnum opus — an objective that entices the vagabond to return and remember its sorcery endlessly time once more.

CHAPTER ONE

Planning Your Trip to Amalfi Coast: A Local's Insight

The Amalfi Coast is a sun-soaked haven where the Mediterranean's allure meets the charm of old towns. Let's get into the intricacies of planning your visit so that you have an unforgettable experience as you embark on this journey.

From exploring the seasons to picking the right convenience and dominating transportation tips, this guide is your visa to capitalizing on your Amalfi experience.

Understanding the Seasons

The Dance of the Seasons

Amalfi in Spring (April to June):

- The coast awakens with vibrant colors as flowers bloom, and temperatures hover between 60°F to 75°F (15°C to 24°C).
- Witness local festivals celebrating spring, such as the Ravello Festival featuring classical music and the Lemon Festival in Amalfi.

Amalfi in Summer (July to August):

- The peak season brings scorching temperatures ranging from 75°F to 90°F (24°C to 32°C).
- Expect bustling crowds and lively beach scenes, making it ideal for sun worshippers and party enthusiasts.

Amalfi in Fall (September to October):

- Mild temperatures around 65°F to 80°F (18°C to 27°C) and a more tranquil atmosphere.
- Enjoy the wine harvest season and local food festivals like the Sagra del Pesce in Positano.

Amalfi in Winter (November to March):

- Quieter streets with temperatures ranging from 50°F to 65°F (10°C to 18°C).
- Some businesses may close during the off-season, but it's an ideal time for a serene, intimate experience.

Navigating Prices

Accommodation Costs: During peak summer, expect higher prices for hotels and rentals. Off-season offers more budget-friendly options with potential discounts, but some amenities may be limited. For example, a hotel room in Positano during summer may range from $300 to $500 per night, while in winter, the cost could decrease to $200 to $400 per night.

Activity Costs: Tour prices may fluctuate. For instance, a boat tour in summer might cost $80–$120, while the same tour in winter could be $60–$90.

Choosing the Right Accommodation

The Amalfi Tapestry: Where to Rest Your Head

Positano's Boutique Charms:

Positano offers boutique hotels with unmatched charm. Consider Hotel Le Agavi on Via Marconi, 127. Nestled along the cliffs, this gem provides a private beach, panoramic views, and a rejuvenating spa. With room rates ranging from $300 to $500 per night, it's a worthwhile investment for an unforgettable stay. When booking, opt for a sea-view room to capture Positano's iconic sunsets. Explore nearby beaches like Spiaggia Grande for a true taste of coastal life.

Example: Hotel Le Agavi

Location: Via Marconi, 127, 84017 Positano SA, Italy.

Contact: +39 089 875 872.

Amenities: Private beach, panoramic views, spa.

Cost: $300–$500 per night.

Tip: Book a sea-view room for breathtaking sunsets, and explore nearby beaches like Spiaggia Grande.

Historic Elegance in Amalfi:

For a taste of historic elegance, look no further than Hotel Santa Caterina on S.S. Amalfitana, 9. With a boundlessness pool, Michelin-featured café, and professional flowerbeds, this Amalfi jewel offers a genuinely vivid encounter. Room rates range from $400 to $800 each evening Choose a cliffside room to wake up to breathtaking views, and don't miss out on the locally inspired dishes at the hotel's restaurant.

Example: Hotel Santa Caterina

Location: S.S. Amalfitana, 9, 84011 Amalfi SA, Italy.

Contact: +39 089 871 012.

Amenities: Infinity pool, Michelin-starred restaurant, botanical gardens.

Cost: $400–$800 per night.

Tip: Opt for a cliffside room for the best views, and indulge in the locally inspired dishes at the hotel's restaurant.

Ravello's Tranquil Retreats:

Ravello, perched high above the sea, beckons with tranquility. Belmond Hotel Caruso on Piazza San Giovanni del Toro, 2, is a retreat of unparalleled luxury. Boasting an infinity pool, wellness center, and garden terrace, it's a haven for relaxation. Room rates range from $600 to $1,200 per night. Take advantage of the wellness offerings, and consider joining a cooking class for an immersive taste of local flavors.

Example: Belmond Hotel Caruso

Location: Piazza San Giovanni del Toro, 2, 84010 Ravello SA, Italy.

Contact: +39 089 858 801.

Amenities: Infinity pool, wellness center, garden terrace.

Cost: $600–$1,200 per night.

Tip: Take advantage of the hotel's wellness offerings and join a cooking class to immerse yourself in local flavors.

Booking Tips

- **Early Reservations:** Secure your accommodation well in advance, especially during peak seasons, to ensure availability and potentially lock in lower rates.
- **Consider Location:** Choose a base that aligns with your interests. Positano for beach life, Amalfi for history, or Ravello for a peaceful escape.

Transportation Tips

Navigating the Coastal Roads

By Car:

- **Rental Cost:** Approximately $50–$100 per day, depending on the type of vehicle.
- The coastal road, Strada Statale 163, offers breathtaking views but requires careful driving due to winding paths.

Public Transportation:

- **Bus Cost:** $2–$5 per journey.
- SITA buses connect major towns, with frequent services. Timetables may vary, so check in advance.

Boat Transfers:

- **Ferry Cost:** $10–$30 per trip.

- Ferries run between towns. Consider a private boat tour for a more personalized experience (around $80–$150 per person).

Amalfi Coast Card

- **Cost:** $30–$50.
- Consider the Amalfi Coast Card, offering unlimited bus rides and discounts on selected attractions.

Exploring on Foot

Hiking Trails: Trails like the Path of the Gods offer stunning views. No cost, but guided tours (around $40–$80) provide insights into local flora and fauna.

Opening and Closing Times

Historical Sites: Museums and historical sites typically open around 9:00 AM and close at 5:00 PM. Check specific sites for exact hours.

Restaurants: Lunch is usually served from 12:30 PM to 2:30 PM, and dinner from 7:30 PM to 10:30 PM. Some establishments close mid-afternoon and reopen for dinner.

As you plan your Amalfi Coast adventure, remember that this region is a living mosaic of history, culture, and natural wonders. By understanding the seasons, choosing the right accommodation, and mastering transportation, you'll unlock the secrets of this coastal gem. Embrace the local rhythms, savor each sunset, and let the magic of the Amalfi Coast unfold before you. Buon viaggio!

CHAPTER TWO

Discovering Amalfi Coast: A Local's Narrative

Welcome to the enchanting Amalfi Coast, a stretch of shoreline where history, beauty, and culture intertwine seamlessly. As a local guide, I invite you to immerse yourself in the allure of Amalfi, Positano, and Ravello, uncover hidden gems off the beaten path, and delve into the cultural richness that defines this coastal haven.

The Enchanting Towns: Amalfi, Positano, Ravello

Amalfi: Where History Meets the Sea

Amalfi Cathedral (Cattedrale di Sant'Andrea):

Location: Piazza Duomo, 84011 Amalfi SA, Italy.

Contact: +39 089 871 286.

Opening Hours: 9:00 AM to 5:00 PM (vary by season).

The Amalfi Cathedral, a jewel of medieval architecture, is a testament and prove to the town's storied past. The entrance fee is approximately $5–$10, providing access to the stunning interiors adorned with intricate mosaics and the Cloister of Paradise. To make the most of your visit, consider guided tours

that offer insights into the cathedral's history and significance. Visit during weekdays to avoid weekend crowds.

Paper Museum (Museo della Carta):

Location: Via delle Cartiere, 24, 84011 Amalfi SA, Italy.

Contact: +39 089 830 4564.

Opening Hours: 10:00 AM to 6:00 PM (closed on Wednesdays).

Amalfi's rich tradition of paper-making comes alive at the Paper Museum. The entrance fee is around $3–$7. Witness the ancient techniques of paper production and explore the museum's collection. Engage with the artisans during demonstrations to gain a deeper appreciation for this local craft. Visit in the morning to experience the museum at a more relaxed pace.

Positano: A Vertical Village of Vibrance

Spiaggia Grande:

Location: 84017 Positano SA, Italy.

Amenities: Public beach, restaurants, beach clubs.

Tip: Arrive early to secure a prime spot on the beach. Rent a beach chair and umbrella for approximately $20–$40 per day.

Indulge in fresh seafood at beachside restaurants like Chez Black. Evening visits offer a romantic atmosphere with the sunset painting the sky.

Path of the Gods (Sentiero degli Dei):

Location: Trailhead near Nocelle, Positano.

Tip: Embark on this panoramic hike early in the morning to avoid the heat. Guided tours, costing around $40–$80, provide insights into local flora and history. Capture stunning coastal views and reach Nocelle for a rewarding lunch at a local trattoria.

Ravello: A Garden Above the Sea

Villa Cimbrone:

Location: Via Santa Chiara, 26, 84010 Ravello SA, Italy.

Contact: +39 089 857 459.

Opening Hours: 9:00 AM to 7:00 PM.

Entrance Fee: $10–$20.

Villa Cimbrone, with its timeless beauty, is a must-visit. Wander through the enchanting gardens, featuring sculptures, fountains, and a terrace with unparalleled views. Engage in a guided tour (approximately $15–$30) to uncover the villa's history. Sunset visits offer a magical experience, but arrive early to explore the gardens in daylight.

Ravello Festival:

Location: Various venues in Ravello.

Tip: Confirm the festival schedules, usually held from June to September, to align your visit with musical performances, concerts, and cultural events. Ticket prices vary, it usually ranges from $30 to $150, depending on the performance and seating.

Hidden Gems Off the Beaten Path

Furore: A Secret Fjord

Fjord di Furore:

Location: Via Marina di Praia, 84010 Furore SA, Italy.

Amenities: Scenic viewpoint, beach access, waterfront restaurants.

Tip: Discover the hidden Fjord di Furore, a secluded cove with crystalline waters. Explore the fjord early in the morning to avoid crowds. Dive into the refreshing sea or savor local seafood at waterfront restaurants like L'Incanto.

Atrani: A Quaint Coastal Escape

Atrani Beach:

Location: 84010 Atrani SA, Italy.

Amenities: Charming town square, beachside cafes.

Tip: Escape the bustling crowds by visiting Atrani. Relax on the small but picturesque Atrani Beach. Explore the quaint town square and savor a leisurely meal at a beachside café like A' Paranza.

Cultural Insights and Local Traditions

The Sounds of Tradition

Tarantella Music and Dance:

Location: Various venues in Amalfi, Positano, and Ravello.

Tip: Immerse yourself in the local culture by attending a Tarantella performance. Check local event calendars for scheduled performances or visit popular spots like Music on the Rocks in Positano. Ticket prices range from $15 to $50, depending on the venue and event.

Sagra Festivals: Celebrating Culinary Heritage

Sagra del Pesce in Positano:

Location: Piazza dei Mulini, Positano.

Tip: Experience local culinary traditions at the Sagra del Pesce (Fish Festival) in Positano. Usually held in September, this festival celebrates the town's fishing heritage. Indulge in freshly caught seafood dishes prepared by local chefs. Prices vary depending on the dishes selected.

Lemon Festival in Amalfi:

Location: Various venues in Amalfi.

Tip: Visit Amalfi in the spring to coincide with the Lemon Festival. Dive into the zesty celebrations with vibrant parades, tastings, and lemon-infused delights. The festival is free to attend, but tasting events may have associated costs.

Artisanal Craft Exploration

Ceramic Workshops in Ravello:

Location: Various artisan workshops in Ravello.

Tip: Ravello is renowned for its exquisite ceramics. Participate in a ceramic workshop (around $30–$60) to try your hand at this traditional craft. Visit workshops like Ceramiche d'Arte Carmela in Ravello to create your personalized ceramic masterpiece.

Embark on a journey through the enchanting towns of Amalfi, Positano, and Ravello, uncover hidden gems off the beaten path, and immerse yourself in the cultural richness of the Amalfi Coast. From exploring historic cathedrals to savoring local cuisine, let each experience be a brushstroke on the canvas of your Amalfi adventure. Discover the magic that lies beyond the postcard-perfect views, and let the heartbeat of this coastal gem guide your exploration. Buon viaggio!

CHAPTER THREE

Savoring the Soul of Amalfi: A Culinary Expedition

Embark on a Gastronomic Odyssey Through the Flavors of the Amalfi Coast. The Amalfi Coast, with its sun-drenched cliffs and cerulean seas, is a haven for those seeking not just breathtaking landscapes but an explosion of flavors that define the essence of Italian cuisine. In the heart of this coastal paradise lies Amalfi, where each bite tells a tale of tradition, passion, and the local way of life. Let's navigate the culinary gems of Amalfi, from hidden trattorias to hands-on cooking experiences.

Exploring Authentic Italian Cuisine

Trattorias and Ristorantes:

To truly understand Amalfi's culinary identity, you must venture beyond the tourist-laden streets and discover the local trattorias that have stood the test of time. One such institution is **"Da Gemma,"** tucked away at Via Fra Gerardo Sasso, 11. Da Gemma is more than just a restaurant; it's a family business that has been around for generations. it's a living demonstration of the district's culinary legacy.

Open for lunch from 12:00 PM to 3:00 PM and for supper from 7:00 PM to 10:30 PM, Da Gemma allures you with its honest façade. As you step onto the porch, the all encompassing perspectives on the Tyrrhenian Ocean set up for an extraordinary eating experience. The menu is a symphony of Amalfitan flavors, but one dish that demands attention is the **"Scialatielli ai Frutti di Mare."** This delectable seafood pasta, priced at $25, showcases the bounty of the Mediterranean on a plate.

Pro Tip: Embrace the local dining rhythm. Lunchtime offers a more laid-back experience, while dinner, especially during sunset, bathes Da Gemma's terrace in a warm, golden glow.

Must-Try Local Dishes and Restaurants:

Lemon-infused Delights:

When in Amalfi, lemons are not just a fruit; they're a way of life. To immerse yourself in this citrus-infused world, head to "Il Gusto della Costa" at Piazza Duomo. This gem not only offers an array of Limoncello variations but also unveils the intricate art of its creation.

The tasting experience, ranging from $15 to $30 per person, is a journey through the tangy and sweet nuances of Amalfi's iconic elixir.

Timing is key here. Visit Il Gusto della Costa in the late afternoon, preferably after 4:00 PM, when the crowds thin out. This allows you not only to enjoy a more intimate tasting but also to engage with the knowledgeable staff, who are eager to share the stories behind each bottle.

Seafood Extravaganza:

For an unabashed celebration of the ocean's bounty, set sail for **"Lo Smeraldino"** at Via Cardinale Marino, 10. This family-owned treasure is a beacon for seafood enthusiasts, and rightly so. The **Grigliata di Pesce** (grilled seafood platter) at $40 is a masterpiece that transcends the concept of a mere meal. Picture this: a table overlooking the azure waters, the aroma of the sea mingling with the sizzle of the grill, and a platter adorned with the freshest catches of the day.

To make the most of your visit, reserve a table for dinner. Aim to arrive around 6:30 PM to secure a spot on the terrace. As the sun dips below the horizon, casting a warm glow on the coastline, you'll understand why Lo Smeraldino is not just a restaurant; it's a sensory journey.

Pro Tip: Engage with the staff. They're not just servers; they're storytellers, ready to guide you through the nuances of each dish and the maritime tales behind them.

Cooking Classes and Food Experiences:

Amalfi Coast Cooking School:

For those yearning to bring a piece of Amalfi's culinary magic back home, the **Amalfi Coast Cooking School** at Via S. Cosma, 4, is a culinary haven. This hands-on experience transcends a typical cooking class; it's an immersion into the soul of Amalfitan cuisine. Classes, spanning around 4 hours, are priced at an average of $100 per person, encompassing all ingredients and a memorable journey through local flavors.

Booking in advance is crucial, especially during peak seasons. Check the schedule on their website and secure your spot early. The intimate setting ensures personalized attention, allowing you to not only learn the art of crafting regional delicacies but also to absorb the passion that fuels Amalfi's culinary traditions.

Local Markets and Tastings:

To witness the pulse of Amalfi's daily life and delve into its culinary treasures, a visit to the Amalfi Market at Piazza Municipio is a must. Elevate this experience with a guided tasting tour by "Taste of Amalfi." The market, open from 8:00 AM to 2:00 PM, is a kaleidoscope of colors and aromas, offering a glimpse into the region's rich produce.

The guided tasting tour, priced at $50 per person, adds a layer of depth to your market exploration. Led by locals passionate about their craft, the tour introduces you to the intricacies of Amalfitan gastronomy. From fresh produce to artisanal cheeses and cured meats, each tasting is a brushstroke on the canvas of Amalfi's culinary artistry.

Pro Tip: Plan your market visit in the morning to witness it in its vibrant glory. Bring a small, eco-friendly bag for any irresistible local finds you might want to take back with you.

Amalfi's culinary landscape is not merely a collection of restaurants; it's a narrative written in flavors, each dish telling a story of tradition, history, and the breathtaking beauty of the Tyrrhenian coastline. As you navigate the trattorias, savor the Limoncello, and immerse yourself in cooking classes, remember that Amalfi's culinary tapestry is not just about taste; it's about capturing the soul of a place through its most intimate rituals. So, embark on this gastronomic odyssey, where every meal is a chapter in the epic tale of Amalfi's culinary legacy.

Beyond the Plate: Immersing in Amalfi's Culinary Tapestry

Wine Tasting in the Vineyards:

To complete your journey through Amalfi's flavors, venture into the hills overlooking the coastline for a wine-tasting experience at "Cantine Marisa Cuomo." Nestled in the dramatic landscape of Furore, this winery crafts wines that reflect the terroir of the region. The cost for a wine tasting session is about $25 per person.

The best chance to visit is throughout the spring and mid year months when the grape plantations are in full blossom. From 10:00 AM to 5:00 PM, the winery is open. Take a directed visit to comprehend the winemaking system and relish their unmistakable whites and reds on a porch that apparently hangs between the sky and the ocean.

Pro Tip: Pair the wines with local cheeses and cured meats for a true Amalfitan experience. Don't rush; let the flavors linger as you soak in the breathtaking views.

Address: Cantine Marisa Cuomo, Via G.B. Lama, 16, 84010 Furore SA, Italy

Contact: +39 089 830348

Website: Cantine Marisa Cuomo

Navigating Culinary Experiences in Amalfi: Practical Tips

Timing Matters:

In Amalfi, time is not just a number; it's an integral part of the experience. Lunchtime offers a more relaxed atmosphere, perfect for soaking in the coastal views without the bustling crowds. Dinner, especially during sunset, transforms the landscape into a canvas painted in hues of gold and orange.

Reservations Are Key:

For popular restaurants like Da Gemma and Lo Smeraldino, reservations are a strategic move, especially for dinner. It ensures you secure the best seats, often on terraces with panoramic views. Make reservations at least a day in advance, and don't be shy to request a table with a view.

Local Conversations:

Engage with locals, be it the chefs, servers, or fellow diners. The stories behind each dish and the traditions woven into the culinary fabric of Amalfi add a layer of richness to your experience. Ask for recommendations, share your culinary preferences, and let the locals guide your gastronomic journey.

Embrace Local Customs:

Limoncello is not just a drink; it's a ritual. When offered at the end of a meal, savor it slowly. The burst of citrus encapsulates the essence of Amalfi. Similarly, when in a trattoria, don't rush. Let the courses unfold, and relish the artistry on your plate.

Pack Light for the Markets:

If you plan to explore the Amalfi Market and indulge in a tasting tour, bring a small, eco-friendly bag. The market is a treasure trove of local products, from handcrafted ceramics to artisanal cheeses, and you might find irresistible souvenirs to take back home.

CHAPTER FOUR

Amalfi Unveiled: Outdoor Adventures Beyond the Horizon

Embarking on Nature's Canvas in the Heart of the Amalfi Coast

While Amalfi is often celebrated for its coastal beauty, the rugged landscapes that cradle this gem also beckon the adventurous spirit. From vertigo-inducing hiking trails that unveil panoramic vistas to aquatic escapades along the coast, Amalfi's outdoor wonders are a testament to nature's artistry. Join me on a journey as we uncover the exhilarating outdoor adventures that await, blending the thrill of exploration with the serene embrace of the Tyrrhenian Sea.

Hiking Trails with Breathtaking Views:

The Sentiero degli Dei (Path of the Gods):

Amalfi's most renowned hiking trail, the Sentiero degli Dei, translates to the "Path of the Gods" and rightfully so. This celestial trail begins in Bomerano (Agerola) and winds its way through lush landscapes, offering awe-inspiring views of the coastline below.

Details:

- **Distance:** Approximately 7.8 kilometers (4.8 miles).
- **Duration:** 3 to 4 hours.
- **Difficulty:** Moderate.

The trail opens at sunrise, presenting a golden opportunity to witness the awakening of the Amalfi Coast.

The panoramic views of the sea, cliffside villages, and distant islands are unparalleled, especially during the early hours when the sunlight bathes the landscape in a warm glow.

- **Cost:** The Sentiero degli Dei is free to access, but consider budgeting around $30 for a guided tour if you prefer local insights and historical context.
- **Pro Tip:** Begin your hike early to avoid the midday heat, and carry a packed lunch to enjoy at one of the scenic viewpoints along the way.

Valle delle Ferriere (Valley of the Ironworks):

For a journey into Amalfi's hinterlands, the Valle delle Ferriere offers a verdant escape. This trail takes you through lemon groves, dense forests, and past ancient ironworks ruins, providing a glimpse into the region's historical and natural wealth.

Details:

- **Distance:** Approximately 6 kilometers (3.7 miles).
- **Duration:** 2 to 3 hours.
- **Difficulty:** Easy to moderate.

The Valle delle Ferriere is open year-round, but spring and autumn unveil the valley in its full splendor. Starting early in the morning allows you to witness the misty enchantment of the valley.

Cost: Access to the trail is free. Guided tours, if desired, may cost around $40 to $60 per person.

Pro Tip: Wear comfortable hiking shoes and pack a camera to capture the vibrant flora and cascading waterfalls along the way.

Water Activities Along the Coast:

Kayaking Along the Amalfi Coast:

To experience Amalfi from a different perspective, embark on a kayaking adventure along its enchanting coastline. **"Amalfi Kayak"** at Marina Grande offers guided kayaking tours, allowing you to paddle through hidden grottoes, beneath natural arches, and along secluded coves.

Details:

- **Duration:** 2 to 3 hours.
- **Availability:** April to October.
- **Skill Level:** Suitable for beginners.

Morning tours, starting around 9:00 AM, ensure calmer waters and the opportunity to witness the sunrise painting the cliffs with hues of pink and gold.

Cost: Kayaking tours typically range from $50 to $80 per person, including equipment and a knowledgeable guide.

Pro Tip: Opt for a small-group tour for a more intimate experience. Capture the best moments by bringing a waterproof camera.

Snorkeling in Conca dei Marini:

Beneath the azure surface of the Tyrrhenian Sea lies a world of vibrant marine life waiting to be explored. The waters near Conca dei Marini, a charming village between Amalfi and Positano, offer excellent snorkeling opportunities.

Details:

- **Best Time to Snorkel:** May to September.
- **Recommended Sites:** Grotta dello Smeraldo and La Galera.
- **Equipment:** Bring your snorkeling gear or rent from local shops.

The underwater caves and rock formations create a captivating underwater landscape. Arrange a boat trip to access the more secluded spots.

Cost: Boat excursions for snorkeling may range from $60 to $100, depending on the duration and inclusions.

Pro Tip: Apply sunscreen generously and wear a rash guard to protect against the sun while snorkeling.

Exploring Nature Reserves:

Monti Lattari Regional Park:

Nature enthusiasts and avid hikers will find solace in the embrace of the Monti Lattari Regional Park.

This expansive reserve, encompassing the mountain range that forms the backbone of the Amalfi Coast, is a treasure trove of biodiversity and breathtaking landscapes.

Details:

- **Access Points:** Various, including Bomerano, Agerola, and Scala.
- **Trails:** Varied difficulty levels, catering to different hiking preferences.
- **Flora and Fauna:** Rich biodiversity, including rare orchids and bird species.

The park is open year-round, but spring and early summer bring an explosion of colors with blooming wildflowers.

Cost: Access to the park is generally free. Guided tours, if desired, may range from $30 to $50 per person.

Pro Tip: Research specific trails based on your fitness level and interests. Don't miss the Valle delle Ferriere trail within the park.

Torre dello Ziro Nature Reserve:

For a journey off the beaten path, explore the Torre dello Ziro Nature Reserve. This hidden gem, perched on the hills above Amalfi, offers a tranquil escape from the bustling coastal towns.

Details:

Access: Via hiking trails from Amalfi or Scala.

Flora and Fauna: A mix of Mediterranean vegetation, including aromatic herbs.

Historical Significance: Ancient watchtowers with panoramic views.

The reserve is open throughout the year, with spring and early autumn providing the most pleasant weather.

Cost: Access is free. Consider hiring a local guide for a more in-depth experience, costing around $40 to $60.

Pro Tip: Pack a picnic and spend a leisurely afternoon at one of the panoramic viewpoints within the reserve.

Amalfi's outdoor wonders are not just about the views; they are about immersing yourself in the raw beauty that defines this coastal marvel. From the dizzying heights of the Sentiero degli Dei to the tranquil depths of the Tyrrhenian Sea, each outdoor adventure unveils a new facet of Amalfi's natural grandeur. So, lace up your hiking boots, grab a paddle, and dive into the embrace of Amalfi's outdoor wonders, where every step and stroke is a dance with nature's symphony.

CHAPTER FIVE

A Stroll Through Time: Unraveling the Art and History of the Amalfi Coast

Tracing the Footsteps of Centuries, Immersed in the Cultural Tapestry. Amalfi, cradled between dramatic cliffs and the Tyrrhenian Sea, breathes life into history's whispers. The amalgamation of architectural wonders, artistic treasures, and cultural legacies creates a symphony that resonates through its streets. Join me on a journey through time as we delve into the art and history that define this coastal haven.

Historical Landmarks and Architecture:

Amalfi Cathedral (Cattedrale di Sant'Andrea):

Nestled at the heart of Amalfi, the Amalfi Cathedral, or Cattedrale di Sant'Andrea, stands as a testament to the town's rich history and architectural prowess. Built in the 9th century, this grand cathedral bears witness to centuries of cultural evolution.

Details:

- **Address:** Piazza Duomo, 84011 Amalfi SA, Italy.
- **Opening Hours:** 9:00 AM to 6:00 PM (Varies seasonally).

- **Entrance Fee:** Approximately $5.

Marvel at the stunning Arab-Norman architecture, characterized by intricate mosaics and a striking façade. To make the most of your visit, consider joining a guided tour. Local guides often infuse historical anecdotes, transforming the stones into storytellers. Venture to the Cloister of Paradise, adjacent to the cathedral, for a serene retreat adorned with medieval frescoes.

Pro Tip: Visit early in the morning or late afternoon to avoid crowds and experience the cathedral in the gentle glow of natural light.

Villa Rufolo:

Perched on a promontory in Ravello, overlooking the Gulf of Salerno, Villa Rufolo is a poetic blend of history, gardens, and breathtaking views. Dating back to the 13th century, this villa has witnessed epochs of artistic inspiration and cultural flourishing.

Details:

- **Address:** Piazza Duomo, 84010 Ravello SA, Italy.
- **Opening Hours:** 9:00 AM to 7:00 PM (Varies seasonally).
- **Entrance Fee:** Approximately $8.

The villa's gardens, adorned with vibrant blooms, offer a sensory journey. Don't miss the panoramic terrace, a muse for Richard Wagner, who found inspiration for his opera Parsifal amidst this coastal Eden.

Pro Tip: Attend a summer concert in the villa's gardens, where music intertwines with the allure of the Amalfi Coast.

Artistic Heritage of Amalfi Coast:

Paper Museum (Museo della Carta):

In the heart of Amalfi, the **Paper Museum** delves into a craft integral to the town's history. Amalfi was a pioneer in paper production, and this museum, housed in an old paper mill, unfolds the artistry and tradition behind the craft.

Details:

Address: Via delle Cartiere, 23, 84011 Amalfi SA, Italy.

Opening Hours: 10:00 AM to 6:00 PM (Closed on Wednesdays).

Entrance Fee: Approximately $4.

Explore the antique machinery and witness paper-making demonstrations. The museum not only preserves the techniques of the past but also fosters contemporary artists who find inspiration in this age-old craft.

Pro Tip: Plan your visit on a sunny day to appreciate the play of light on the translucent paper, creating a magical ambiance within the museum.

San Francesco Church and Cloister:

Beyond the hustle of the main square in Sorrento, the San Francesco Church beckons with a serene allure. Dating back to the

14th century, this church and its cloister encapsulate the spiritual and artistic essence of the Amalfi Coast.

Details:

- **Address:** Piazza Francesco Saverio Gargiulo, 1, 80067 Sorrento NA, Italy.
- **Opening Hours:** 8:00 AM to 12:00 PM, 4:00 PM to 8:00 PM.
- **Entrance Fee:** Approximately $2.

The cloister, adorned with majolica tiles and a lush garden, provides a tranquil escape from the vibrant streets. Admire the detailed frescoes in the church that narrate biblical stories with a touch of local flavor.

Pro Tip: Attend an evening concert in the cloister during the summer months, where the acoustics enhance the magic of the performance.

Museums and Galleries:

Museum of Wood Inlay (Museo della Civiltà Contadina):

In the quaint village of Scala, the Museum of Wood Inlay pays homage to the intricate craftsmanship that defines the region. Explore the evolution of woodwork, from everyday objects to ornate furniture, in a charming setting that reflects the rustic charm of rural life.

Details:

- **Address:** Via del Santo, 10, 84010 Scala SA, Italy.
- **Opening Hours:** 10:00 AM to 1:00 PM, 3:00 PM to 7:00 PM (Closed on Mondays).
- **Entrance Fee:** Approximately $5.

The museum's collection is a journey through time, showcasing the skill of local artisans. Engage with the knowledgeable staff who provide insights into the techniques and stories behind each piece.

Pro Tip: Combine your visit with a stroll through the picturesque streets of Scala, offering a glimpse into authentic Amalfitan life.

Contemporary Art at Fondazione Sorrento:

For a brushstroke of modernity amid historic treasures, the Fondazione Sorrento is a haven for contemporary art enthusiasts. Located in the heart of Sorrento, this gallery hosts rotating exhibitions that showcase the work of local and international artists.

Details:

- **Address:** Via S. Antonio, 19/21, 80067 Sorrento NA, Italy.
- **Opening Hours:** 10:00 AM to 6:00 PM (Closed on Mondays).
- **Entrance Fee:** Approximately $7.

The gallery's minimalist design allows the artwork to take center stage. Attend one of their exhibition openings to engage with artists and fellow art enthusiasts.

Pro Tip: Check the exhibition schedule in advance, and plan your visit around an artist talk or special event for a more immersive experience.

Amalfi's art and history are not confined to the pages of a book; they echo through the cobblestone streets, resonate in the grandeur of cathedrals, and whisper in the rustling leaves of centuries-old gardens. Whether you're tracing the footsteps of medieval craftsmen in the Paper Museum or immersing yourself in the contemporary beats of Fondazione Sorrento, each exploration is a brushstroke on the canvas of Amalfi's cultural legacy. So, step into the past, linger in the present, and let the art and history of the Amalfi Coast unfold before you in a symphony of colors, textures, and stories.

CHAPTER SIX

Amalfi Nights: A Symphony of Entertainment and Enchantment

From Sunset Serenades to Hidden Haunts, Unravel the Nightlife Tapestry of the Amalfi Coast. As the sun dips below the horizon, the Amalfi Coast undergoes a captivating metamorphosis.

The quaint villages and lively towns transform into stages where the night unfolds with a blend of tradition and contemporary allure. Join me as we navigate the vibrant nightlife of the Amalfi Coast, exploring the beats, melodies, and unique spaces that come alive after sunset.

Vibrant Night Scenes in Amalfi Coast:

Piazza Duomo - Amalfi's Heartbeat:

In the heart of Amalfi lies the pulsating nucleus of the town's nightlife – Piazza Duomo. As day turns to night, this central square becomes a meeting point for locals and visitors alike. Surrounded by historic buildings, lively cafés, and the stunning Amalfi Cathedral, Piazza Duomo is the epicenter of Amalfi's evening charm.

Details:

Location: Piazza Duomo, 84011 Amalfi SA, Italy.

As the clock strikes 7:00 PM, the square comes alive. Grab a seat at one of the outdoor cafés like Bar Pasticceria Savoia or Gran Caffè, Pansa, where you can sip on a classic Aperol Spritz or a locally crafted limoncello. The atmosphere is electric, especially during the summer months when live music performances often grace the square.

Pro Tip: Arrive early to secure a prime seat, and relish the transition from dusk to night as the cathedral is subtly illuminated.

Marina Grande - Positano's Coastal Elegance:

Positano, with its pastel-hued houses cascading down the cliffs, unveils a different allure come nighttime. Marina Grande, the main beach area, transforms into a picturesque setting for an evening by the sea.

Details:

Location: Marina Grande, 84017 Positano SA, Italy.

As the sun sets, the beachside restaurants and bars like Chez Black and Ristorante C'era una Volta illuminate the shoreline. Dive into the enchanting ambiance with a seaside dinner and linger as live music often drifts through the air. The gentle lapping of the waves adds a soothing rhythm to the evening.

Pro Tip: Combine dinner with a stroll along the beach to fully absorb the romantic atmosphere, and don't be afraid to ask locals for recommendations on the best spots for live music.

Live Music and Events:

Music Under the Stars at Villa Rufolo - Ravello's Cultural Oasis:

Ravello, perched high above the coast, offers a cultural haven that transcends the typical nightlife experience. The Villa Rufolo Concert Series transforms the historic gardens into an open-air auditorium, where classical and contemporary melodies reverberate against the backdrop of the Tyrrhenian Sea.

Details:

- **Location:** Villa Rufolo, Piazza Duomo, 1, 84010 Ravello SA, Italy.
- **Event Schedule:** Check the official website for upcoming concerts.

The concert series, which typically runs from late spring to early autumn, features renowned artists and orchestras. Imagine sitting under the stars, surrounded by lush greenery, as the notes of a Chopin nocturne or a Puccini aria fill the air.

- **Cost:** Ticket prices vary but generally range from $30 to $100, depending on the artist and seating.

Pro Tip: Book tickets well in advance, and consider opting for a VIP or premium seating option for an enhanced experience.

Music on the Rocks - Positano's Cliffside Rhythms:

For those seeking a more contemporary vibe, Music on the Rocks in Positano is an iconic nightclub that rocks the cliffs. Carved into the rugged rocks of the Amalfi Coast, this venue hosts energetic DJ sets and live performances, making it a magnet for night owls.

Details:

- **Location:** Vla Grotte dell'Incanto, 51, 84017 Positano SA, Italy.
- **Opening Hours:** 10:00 PM to 3:00 AM.
  The club, set against the natural caves, offers a panoramic dance floor overlooking the sea. The energy here is infectious, with the music blending seamlessly with the crashing waves below.
- **Cost:** Entry fees range from $20 to $50, and table reservations may require additional charges.

Pro Tip: Arrive fashionably late, around 11:30 PM, to catch the party at its peak. Dress to impress, and don't forget your dancing shoes.

Unique Bars and Cafés:

Franco's Bar - Aperitivo Elegance in Positano:

Positano boasts a gem hidden in plain sight – **Franco's Bar**, an epitome of sophistication and charm. Perched above the town, this bar offers unparalleled views of the sunset over the Tyrrhenian Sea.

Details:

- **Location:** Piazzetta dei Mulini, 50, 84017 Positano SA, Italy.
- **Opening Hours:** 5:00 PM to 12:00 AM.

Franco's Bar is renowned for its impeccable service and a curated menu of signature cocktails. Savor the renowned Positano Sunset, a concoction of local ingredients that perfectly complements the stunning panorama.

Cost: Cocktails range from $15 to $20, and the experience is well worth the investment.

Pro Tip: Opt for the Aperitivo Hour (6:00 PM to 8:00 PM) to enjoy complimentary snacks with your drinks, enhancing the overall experience.

Grotta dello Smeraldo - Subterranean Magic in Conca dei Marini:

For a unique drinking experience, venture into the Grotta dello Smeraldo, a mesmerizing sea cave in Conca dei Marini. The cave houses a bar where you can sip your favorite drink surrounded by the emerald glow of the underwater cavern.

Details:

- **Location:** Via Grotta dello Smeraldo, 84010 Conca dei Marini SA, Italy.
- **Opening Hours:** 10:00 AM to 5:00 PM (Boat ride to the cave).

Accessed by a short boat ride from the Amalfi Coast, the Grotta dello Smeraldo is a hidden treasure. The unique lighting within the cave creates an otherworldly atmosphere, making it an ideal spot for a pre-dinner aperitivo.

Cost: Boat rides to the cave may cost around $10 to $20, and drinks at the cave bar are reasonably priced.

Pro Tip: Plan your visit during the late afternoon to witness the changing colors of the cave as the sunlight filters through the water.

The nightlife of the Amalfi Coast is a harmonious fusion of tradition and contemporary allure. From the lively squares of Amalfi to the cliffside beats of Positano, each venue and event is a note in the symphony of the night. So, as the sun sets over the Tyrrhenian Sea, let the enchantment of the Amalfi Coast's evenings sweep you into a world where every corner holds a melody, every sip tells a story, and every moment becomes a timeless memory.

0

CHAPTER SEVEN

Navigating the Amalfi Coast: A Local's Guide to Practical Wisdom

From Fiscal Frugality to Cultural Compass, Unveiling the Secrets of Seamless Sojourning

Embarking on an Amalfi Coast adventure isn't merely about the picturesque landscapes and tantalizing cuisine; it's a journey woven with practicalities and cultural nuances. Let's delve into the heart of practical wisdom, unraveling the secrets that transform your sojourn into an effortless exploration of this coastal haven.

Money-Saving Strategies:

Dining Delights without Breaking the Bank:

Savoring the culinary wonders of the Amalfi Coast need not empty your pockets. While the coastal eateries exude charm, consider exploring the local trattorias and osterias for authentic flavors without the hefty price tag. Venture away from the main tourist hubs, and you'll find hidden gems where locals gather for their daily feasts.

Examples:

Trattoria Da Ciccio in Positano (Via Laurito, 43, 84017 Positano SA, Italy) offers delectable seafood dishes at reasonable prices.

Il Ritrovo in Ravello (Via Pantaleone Comite, 33, 84010 Ravello SA, Italy) is renowned for its traditional Southern Italian cuisine without the upscale cost.

Average Cost: A meal at a local trattoria can range from $20 to $40 per person, significantly more budget-friendly than some high-profile restaurants.

Pro Tip: Opt for the "Menu del Giorno" or daily specials, often a more economical choice offering a taste of local favorites.

Budget-Friendly Accommodations with Coastal Charm:

Amalfi's cliffside elegance doesn't solely belong to luxury hotels. Embrace the coastal spirit without breaking the bank by considering charming bed-and-breakfasts and family-run guesthouses. Places like Villa Maria Antonietta in Amalfi (Via Maestra dei Villaggi, 34, 84011 Amalfi SA, Italy) offer a warm, local experience without sacrificing comfort.

Average Cost: Budget accommodations can range from $70 to $150 per night, depending on the season and specific location.

Pro Tip: Plan your stay during the shoulder seasons (spring and fall) for more affordable rates and fewer crowds.

Cost-Effective Transportation:

While the allure of the Amalfi Coast lies in its cliffside drives, renting a car may not always be the most budget-friendly option. Instead, rely on the efficient and picturesque public transportation. The SITA bus system connects the coastal towns, providing a cost-effective and scenic journey. Additionally, ferries are a delightful way to hop between towns while enjoying the coastal views.

Average Cost: A one-way SITA bus ticket can cost around $2 to $5, and ferry rides may range from $10 to $20, depending on the distance.

Pro Tip: Purchase a multi-day or multi-ride pass for the SITA bus to save on transportation costs, and be sure to check the ferry schedule for convenient timings.

Safety Precautions:

Navigating the Coastal Roads with Caution:

The Amalfi Coast's serpentine roads, while offering breathtaking views, demand cautious driving. If renting a car, ensure you are comfortable with narrow and winding routes. Consider opting for a smaller vehicle, and if the roads seem daunting, rely on local drivers or public transportation.

Safety Measures:

- **Drive during daylight hours whenever possible to enhance visibility.**
- **Be vigilant of oncoming traffic, especially around blind curves.**
- **Utilize designated parking areas to avoid roadside hazards.**

Pro Tip: If driving seems intimidating, hire a local driver for day trips, providing both safety and the chance to soak in the scenery.

Water Safety for Aquatic Adventures:

Whether indulging in a boat tour or a swim along the coast, prioritize water safety. Confirm that your chosen boat tour operator adheres to safety standards and provides life jackets. If swimming in the sea, choose designated swimming areas and be mindful of currents.

Safety Measures:

- Wear a life jacket during boat tours, especially if venturing into grottoes or caves.
- Swim in designated areas with lifeguards, and avoid areas with strong currents.
- Stay informed about weather conditions, as the sea can become unpredictable.

Pro Tip: If you're not a strong swimmer, consider a guided boat tour that includes snorkeling, ensuring a safe and enjoyable experience.

Beware of Pickpockets in Crowded Areas:

While the Amalfi Coast exudes a sense of safety, crowded tourist spots can attract pickpockets. Exercise caution in bustling areas like Piazza Duomo in Amalfi or Spiaggia Grande in Positano. Use anti-theft accessories, such as money belts, and be vigilant in crowded places.

Safety Measures:

- Keep valuables secured in anti-theft bags or money belts.
- Avoid displaying large amounts of cash or expensive belongings.
- Be cautious when approached by overly friendly strangers in crowded areas.

Pro Tip: Split your money and belongings, storing them in different places, to minimize the impact of potential theft.

Language and Local Etiquette:

The Italian Essentials:

While English is commonly spoken in tourist areas, mastering a few Italian phrases can enhance your experience and foster connections with locals. Simple greetings, "Grazie" (thank you), and "Per favore" (please) go a long way. Italians appreciate visitors who make an effort to embrace their language and culture.

Local Phrases:

- Buongiorno (bwohn-johr-noh): Good morning.
- Buonasera (bwoh-nah-seh-rah): Good evening.
- Posso avere il conto, per favore? (pohs-soh ah-vehr-eh eel kohn-toh, pehr fah-voh-reh): Can I have the bill, please?

Pro Tip: Download a language app or carry a pocket phrasebook for quick reference and language support.

Respecting Local Customs:

Amalfi Coast residents take pride in their cultural heritage, and respecting local customs enhances your travel experience. When entering churches or religious sites, dress modestly. Additionally, it's customary to greet people with a handshake and make eye contact during conversations.

Local Customs:

- Cover shoulders and knees when visiting religious sites.
- Greet locals with a handshake and maintain eye contact during conversations.
- Avoid loud conversations or disruptive behavior in public spaces.

Pro Tip: Familiarize yourself with basic Italian dining etiquette, such as not asking for Parmesan cheese on seafood dishes, to seamlessly blend in with local dining traditions.

Understanding the Siesta Culture:

The concept of "siesta," an afternoon break or nap, is ingrained in the Italian way of life. Many businesses, especially smaller shops and family-run establishments, may close during the early afternoon hours. Plan your activities accordingly, ensuring you don't find yourself in need of services during siesta time.

Sieta Timing:

Siesta typically occurs from 1:00 PM to 4:00 PM.

Avoid scheduling important appointments or visits during these hours.

Pro Tip: Embrace the siesta culture by enjoying a leisurely lunch during this time, allowing you to recharge before afternoon activities resume.

As you embark on your Amalfi Coast adventure, let practical wisdom be your trusted guide. From savoring local delicacies without draining your wallet to navigating coastal roads with caution, every practical tip weaves seamlessly into the fabric of your journey. Embrace the nuances of language, adhere to safety precautions, and dance through the coastal villages with a cultural compass. In the end, it's these practical insights that transform your visit from a mere vacation into an immersive, authentic experience along the breathtaking shores of the Amalfi Coast.

CHAPTER EIGHT

A Day Tripper's Odyssey: Unveiling the Secrets of Capri, Pompeii, and Beyond

Embark on a Journey Beyond the Horizon, Where Every Day Trip Unfolds a New Tale. The allure of the Amalfi Coast extends far beyond its sun-kissed shores and charming villages. Day trips and excursions unveil hidden gems, ancient wonders, and panoramic vistas that linger in memory. Join me as we embark on a day-tripper's odyssey, exploring the secrets of Capri, the buried cities of Pompeii and Herculaneum, and uncovering insider tips to make each excursion an unforgettable chapter in your coastal adventure.

Capri Island Escape:
A Ferry Ride into Paradise:

As the sun paints the Tyrrhenian Sea with hues of azure, embark on a ferry ride from the Amalfi Coast to the enchanting island of Capri. Ferries depart regularly from Positano, Amalfi, and Sorrento, offering a scenic voyage with the iconic Faraglioni rocks welcoming you to Capri's embrace.

Ferry Operators:

- **Cooperativa Sant'Andrea:** Offers daily departures from Positano.
- **Travelmar:** Connects Amalfi with Capri with a comfortable ferry service.
- **Consorzio Marittimo Turistico**: Provides ferry options from Sorrento.

Average Cost: Ferry tickets range from $20 to $40 one-way, depending on the departure point and type of vessel.

Pro Tip: Opt for an early morning ferry to capture the sunrise over the sea and secure a comfortable seat on the open deck.

Anacapri's Tranquil Charms:

Upon arriving in Capri, resist the allure of the bustling main square and set your sights on Anacapri, the quieter sibling perched at a higher altitude. Reach Anacapri by bus or the iconic chairlift from Piazza della Vittoria, where sweeping views of the coastline accompany you to the summit.

Chairlift Operator:

Seggiovia Monte Solaro: Offers chairlift rides from Anacapri to Mount Solaro.

Average Cost: Chairlift tickets are approximately $15 to $20, providing a breathtaking ascent.

Pro Tip: Choose a clear day for the chairlift ride to enjoy unobstructed views of the Gulf of Naples and the Amalfi Coast.

Villa San Michele - A Garden of Dreams:

Nestled in Anacapri, the Villa San Michele is a testament to the vision of Swedish physician Axel Munthe. Explore this dream-like villa and its lush gardens, adorned with ancient artifacts and vibrant flora. The views from the terrace are postcard-perfect, offering glimpses of Capri's coastline.

Details:

- **Address:** Viale Axel Munthe, 34, 80071 Anacapri NA, Italy.
- **Opening Hours:** 9:00 AM to 6:00 PM (Varies seasonally).
- **Entrance Fee:** Approximately $10 to $15.

Pro Tip: Visit during the late afternoon when the sunlight bathes the gardens in a warm glow, creating a magical ambiance.

Faraglioni Boat Tour - Coastal Majesty Unveiled:

Cap off your Capri adventure with a boat tour around the Faraglioni rocks, the iconic limestone formations that define Capri's coastal allure. Numerous boat operators offer tours, allowing you to sail through natural arches and grottoes, with the Faraglioni towering majestically in the background.

Boat Tour Operators:

- **Motoscafisti di Capri:** Offers small group tours with knowledgeable guides.

- **Gianni's Boat:** Provides private boat charters for a personalized experience.

Average Cost: Boat tours range from $40 to $80, depending on the duration and type of tour.

Pro Tip: Choose a small group tour for a more intimate experience and the opportunity to access hidden grottoes.

Pompeii and Herculaneum Explorations:

A Time Capsule Unearthed: Pompeii:

Embark on a journey through time as you explore the ancient city of Pompeii, frozen in the moment of its catastrophic demise in 79 AD. Walk the cobbled streets, marvel at the remarkably preserved frescoes, and stand in the amphitheater where the echoes of ancient spectacles linger.

Site Details:

Address: Pompei, Province of Naples, Italy.

- **Opening Hours:** 9:00 AM to 7:00 PM (Varies seasonally).
- **Entrance Fee:** Approximately $20 to $25.
- **Pro Tip**: Engage a licensed guide at the entrance for a richer experience, unraveling the stories behind the ruins.

Herculaneum - A Lesser-Known Gem:

While Pompeii takes the spotlight, nearby Herculaneum offers a more intimate glimpse into ancient Roman life. Smaller and better preserved due to the layers of volcanic ash, Herculaneum's villas, mosaics, and even wooden furniture provide an unparalleled view into daily life.

Site Details:

- **Address:** Ercolano, Metropolitan City of Naples, Italy.
- **Opening Hours:** 9:00 AM to 7:00 PM (Varies seasonally).
- **Entrance Fee:** Approximately $15 to $20.

Mount Vesuvius - A Volcanic Odyssey:

Delegated the Narrows of Naples, Mount Vesuvius entices swashbucklers to climb its inclines for an all encompassing perspective on the tremendous scene underneath. Start your excursion at the Vesuvius Public Park, where a winding way drives you to the cavity's edge, offering a remarkable viewpoint on the scandalous well of lava that eternity modified the direction of history.

Details:

- **Address:** Via Palazzo del Principe, 1, 80044 Ottaviano NA, Italy.
- **Opening Hours**: 9:00 AM to 3:00 PM (Varies seasonally).
- **Entrance Fee:** Approximately $10 to $15.

Pro Tip: Wear comfortable shoes and carry water, as the ascent can be steep, but the unparalleled views from the summit are well worth the effort.

Sorrento - Gateway to the Past:

Wrap up your Pompeii and Herculaneum explorations with a leisurely stroll through Sorrento. This charming town, perched atop the cliffs overlooking the Bay of Naples, provides a perfect setting for reflection after a day immersed in ancient history.

Pro Tip: While there isn't a specific entrance fee for Sorrento, allocate time to wander through the historic center, enjoy a gelato at Piazza Tasso, and soak in the breathtaking views from the Villa Comunale park.

Insider Tips for Day Trips:

Off-Peak Bliss:

To fully relish the charm of Capri and the archaeological wonders of Pompeii and Herculaneum, consider planning your day trips during the shoulder seasons—spring and fall. The weather is pleasant, crowds are thinner, and you'll have a more immersive experience without the summer rush.

Pro Tip: Aim for mid-week visits to further avoid crowds, allowing you to explore each site at your own pace.

Early Bird Catches the View:

For those embarking on the Capri chairlift adventure or hoping to catch the sunrise over the Amalfi Coast, an early start is your golden ticket. Beat the crowds, witness the coast bathed in morning light, and relish moments of solitude before the day unfolds.

Pro Tip: Arrive at chairlift stations or scenic viewpoints at least 30 minutes before opening to secure prime spots.

Guided Insights:

While independent exploration holds its charm, consider engaging local guides for certain excursions, especially in Pompeii and Herculaneum. Licensed guides offer invaluable insights, untold stories, and a deeper understanding of the historical context, transforming your visit into an educational and immersive experience.

Pro Tip: Join group tours for cost-effectiveness or opt for private guides for a personalized journey tailored to your interests.

Dine Like a Local:

In Capri and along the Amalfi Coast, veer away from tourist-centric eateries and savor the local culinary delights. Seek recommendations from residents or explore narrow alleys to discover hidden trattorias and family-run gems. Not only will you enjoy more authentic flavors, but you'll also likely find more budget-friendly options.

Pro Tip: Ask locals for their favorite spots and embrace the traditional Amalfitan dishes for a genuine taste of the region.

As you venture beyond the enchanting villages of the Amalfi Coast, each day trip becomes a chapter in a riveting narrative of history, beauty, and exploration. From the heights of Capri to the preserved streets of Pompeii and the timeless allure of Sorrento, these excursions offer a multifaceted glimpse into the soul of southern Italy. Armed with insider tips, embrace the rhythm of local life, allowing each day trip to unfold like a well-crafted story—a tale you'll carry with you long after the echoes of your footsteps have faded away.

CHAPTER NINE

Festivals and Events

The Amalfi Coast, with its dramatic cliffs and cerulean waters, is not only a visual feast but also a cultural tapestry woven with vibrant festivals and events. Join me as we embark on a journey through time, exploring annual celebrations deeply rooted in history, discovering how to immerse yourself in local festivities, and unveiling the anticipated event calendar for the year 2024.

Annual Celebrations in Amalfi Coast:

Feast of Saint Andrew - Amalfi's Maritime Legacy:

In the heart of Amalfi, where history whispers through narrow alleys and ancient cathedrals, the Feast of Saint Andrew stands as a testament to the city's maritime heritage. Celebrated on November 30th, this event commemorates the patron saint of fishermen, Saint Andrew.

Event Highlights:

- **Religious Procession:** Watch as the statue of Saint Andrew is paraded through the streets, accompanied by the rhythmic sounds of local bands.

- **Historical Reenactments:** Experience Amalfi's maritime past with reenactments of historical events, showcasing the city's connection to the sea.

Pro Tip: Secure a spot along the procession route early to witness the grandeur of the religious spectacle.

Ravello Festival - Harmony in the Hills:

As summer casts its golden glow over the Amalfi Coast, the hills of Ravello come alive with the enchanting melodies of the Ravello Festival. Running from June to September, this renowned event transforms historic venues into stages for world-class music, dance, and theatrical performances.

Event Highlights:

- **Open-Air Concerts:** Revel in the magical atmosphere of open-air concerts held in iconic locations such as Villa Rufolo and the Auditorium Oscar Niemeyer.
- **Cultural Workshops:** Immerse yourself in the arts with workshops ranging from traditional ceramics to contemporary dance.
- **Ticket Prices:** Concert tickets vary, ranging from $30 for basic seats to $150 for premium experiences.

Pro Tip: Check the festival schedule in advance and book tickets for your preferred performances to secure the best seats.

Lemon Festival - Citrus Extravaganza in Minori:

As winter bids farewell, the town of Minori bursts into a riot of colors with the Lemon Festival, celebrated in late spring. This lively event pays homage to the Amalfi Coast's iconic produce—the Amalfi lemon.

Event Highlights:

- **Parades and Floats:** Marvel at colorful parades featuring floats adorned with lemons of all shapes and sizes, showcasing the craftsmanship of the locals.
- **Citrus Market:** Explore the vibrant market offering an array of lemon-inspired products, from limoncello to lemon-infused sweets.

Pro Tip: Visit local pastry shops during the festival to savor traditional lemon-flavored delicacies crafted specifically for the occasion.

Participating in Local Festivities:

Immerse in Religious Traditions:

Amalfi's religious festivals, deeply ingrained in local culture, offer a unique window into the community's spirituality and heritage. Whether it's the Easter processions, Corpus Domini celebrations, or the Feast of Saint Andrew, participating in these religious events provides a profound connection to the soul of the Amalfi Coast.

Participation Tips:

- **Respectful Attire:** When attending religious events, dress modestly as a sign of respect for the sacred nature of the occasion.
- **Learn Local Customs:** Familiarize yourself with the customs associated with each festival, such as offering flowers during religious processions.

Engage in Culinary Extravaganzas:

Food is at the heart of Amalfi's cultural identity, and festivals often showcase the region's rich gastronomic heritage. From the Sagra del Pesce (Fish Festival) to the Festa di San Michele Arcangelo, immerse yourself in the culinary delights that define each celebration.

Participation Tips:

- **Sample Local Specialties**: Take advantage of festival-specific dishes, often crafted using traditional recipes passed down through generations.
- **Join Cooking Classes:** Some festivals offer cooking classes, providing an opportunity to learn the secrets of Amalfitan cuisine from local chefs.

Connect Through Local Arts and Crafts:

Many festivals feature vibrant markets where local artisans display their crafts, from handmade ceramics to intricate lacework. Engage with these artisans, learn about their techniques, and acquire unique souvenirs that encapsulate the spirit of the Amalfi Coast.

Participation Tips:

- **Support Local Artisans:** Purchase directly from artisans to support the local economy and acquire one-of-a-kind, handmade treasures.
- **Attend Workshops:** Some festivals organize workshops where visitors can try their hand at traditional crafts under the guidance of skilled artisans.

Event Calendar for 2024:

January to March:

Easter Celebrations (April 1, 2024): Experience the elaborate processions and religious festivities marking Easter, a significant event in Amalfi's calendar.

April to June:

- **Lemon Festival in Minori (Late May):** Dive into a citrus-filled extravaganza with parades, markets, and the vibrant spirit of spring.
- **Amalfi Historic Regatta (June 17, 2024):** Witness historic boats race along the Amalfi coastline in a celebration of maritime heritage.

July to September:

Ravello Festival (June to September): Immerse yourself in a cultural feast featuring music, dance, and art in the idyllic setting of Ravello.

Atrani Music Festival (August 10-15, 2024): Delight in classical and contemporary music performances in the charming village of Atrani.

October to December:

- **Sorrento Tarantella Festival (October 12-14, 2024):** Join the lively festivities celebrating the traditional tarantella dance in the captivating town of Sorrento.
- **Christmas Markets in Amalfi (December):** Embrace the holiday spirit with festive markets, illuminations, and seasonal treats.

Pro Tip: Plan your visit around specific festivals or events to add an extra layer of cultural richness to your Amalfi Coast experience.

In the heart of the Amalfi Coast, every festival and event is a chapter in a timeless narrative—where traditions echo through the cobblestone streets, music resonates in historic venues, and the zest of lemons infuses the air. As you weave through the tapestry of celebrations, let the rhythmic beats of local music and the vibrant colors of festivals become an integral part of your own Amalfitan story—one that unfolds with each spirited gathering along this captivating stretch of the Italian coastline.

AMALFI COAST MAP

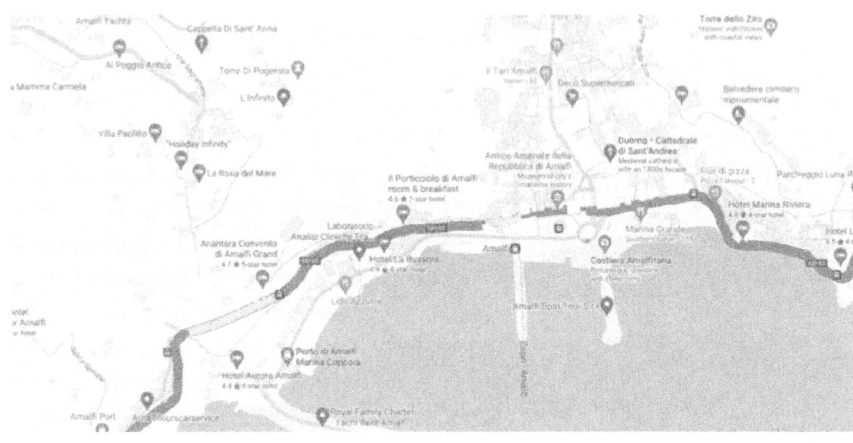

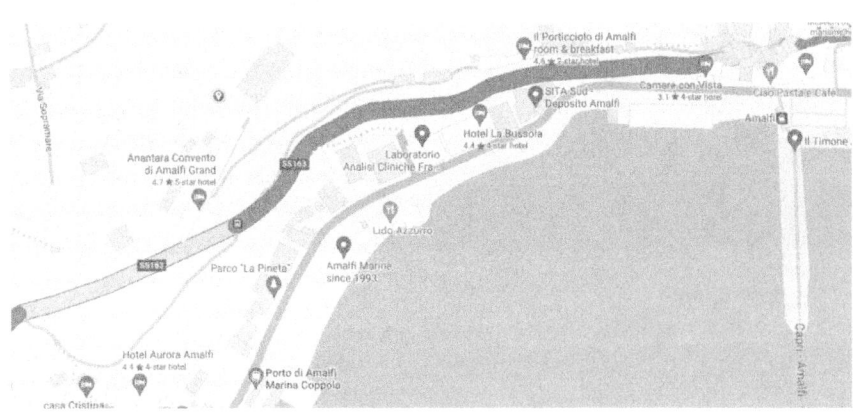

CONCLUSION

We are on the verge of an adventure that goes beyond the pages of our "Travel Guide to Amalfi Coast 2024" as the final chapter draws to a close. The Amalfi Coast is waiting for you to explore, with its stunning landscapes, intricate cultural tapestry, and lively festivals.

In this guide, we've journeyed through the winding streets of ancient villages, tasted the flavors of locally-inspired cuisine, stood witness to the echoes of history in ruins, and danced to the rhythms of lively festivals. Each page turned has been a step closer to unraveling the secrets of the Amalfi Coast, revealing not just its scenic beauty but also the heartbeat of its communities.

As you prepare for your sojourn along the cliffs and coves, remember that this guide is merely a compass. The true magic lies in the moments of spontaneity, in the unplanned detours that lead to hidden gems, and in the connections forged with the welcoming locals.

May your exploration of the Amalfi Coast be filled with sun-soaked days and moonlit nights, where every sunset paints the sea in hues of gold and every dawn brings the promise of new discoveries. Whether you find yourself immersed in the ancient history of Pompeii, savoring the zest of Amalfi lemons, or losing track of time amidst the melodies of Ravello, let this guide be your companion in crafting an unforgettable journey.

In the spirit of discovery, adventure, and cultural immersion, may your travels along the Amalfi Coast in 2024 be nothing short of a captivating odyssey—one that lingers in your heart long after the echoes of your footsteps have faded away.

Safe travels and embrace the magic of the Amalfi Coast!

AMALFI COAST
TRAVEL JOURNAL 2024

NAPLES TRAVEL JOURNAL 2024

NAPLES TRAVEL JOURNAL 2024

NAPLES TRAVEL JOURNAL 2024

NAPLES TRAVEL JOURNAL 2024

NAPLES TRAVEL JOURNAL 2024

Printed in Great Britain
by Amazon

43651172R00056